SCHOLASTIC
READ & RESPOND

Bringing the best books to life in the classroom

Activities based on Aliens Love Underpants
By Claire Freedman

Terms and conditions

IMPORTANT – PERMITTED USE AND WARNINGS – READ CAREFULLY BEFORE USING

Copyright in the software contained in this CD-ROM and in its accompanying material belongs to Scholastic Limited. All rights reserved. © 2016 Scholastic Ltd.

Save for these purposes, or as expressly authorised in the accompanying materials, the software may not be copied, reproduced, used, sold, licensed, transferred, exchanged, hired, or exported in whole or in part or in any manner or form without the prior written consent of Scholastic Ltd. Any such unauthorised use or activities are prohibited and may give rise to civil liabilities and criminal prosecutions.

The material contained on this CD-ROM may only be used in the context for which it was intended in *Read & Respond*, and is for use only by the purchaser or purchasing institution that has purchased the book and CD-ROM. Permission to download images is given for purchasers only and not for users from any lending service. Any further use of the material contravenes Scholastic Ltd's copyright and that of other rights holders.

This CD-ROM has been tested for viruses at all stages of its production. However, we recommend that you run virus-checking software on your computer systems at all times. Scholastic Ltd cannot accept any responsibility for any loss, disruption or damage to your data or your computer system that may occur as a result of using either the CD-ROM or the data held on it.

IF YOU ACCEPT THE ABOVE CONDITIONS YOU MAY PROCEED TO USE THE CD-ROM.

Recommended system requirements:
Windows: XP (Service Pack 3), Vista (Service Pack 2), Windows 7 or Windows 8 with 2.33GHz processor
Mac: OS 10.6 to 10.8 with Intel Core™ Duo processor
1GB RAM (recommended)
1024 x 768 Screen resolution
CD-ROM drive (24x speed recommended)
Adobe Reader (version 9 recommended for Mac users)
Broadband internet connections (for installation and updates)

For all technical support queries (including no CD drive), please phone Scholastic Customer Services on 0845 6039091.

Designed using Adobe Indesign
Published by Scholastic Education, an imprint of Scholastic Ltd
Book End, Range Road, Witney, Oxfordshire, OX29 0YD
Registered office: Westfield Road, Southam,
Warwickshire CV47 0RA

Printed and bound by Ashford Colour Press
© 2016 Scholastic Ltd
123456789 6789012345

British Library Cataloguing-in-Publication Data
A catalogue record for this book is available from the British Library.
ISBN 978-1407-14227-2

All rights reserved. This book is sold subject to the condition that it shall not, by way of trade or otherwise, be lent, hired out or otherwise circulated without the publisher's prior consent in any form of binding or cover other than that in which it is published and without a similar condition, including this condition, being imposed upon the subsequent purchaser.

No part of this publication may be reproduced, stored in a retrieval system, or transmitted, in any form or by any means, electronic, mechanical, photocopying, recording or otherwise, other than for the purposes described in the lessons in this book, without the prior permission of the publisher. This book remains copyright, although permission is granted to copy pages where indicated for classroom distribution and use only in the school which has purchased the book, or by the teacher who has purchased the book, and in accordance with the CLA licensing agreement. Photocopying permission is given only for purchasers and not for borrowers of books from any lending service.

Extracts from *The National Curriculum in England, English Programme of Study* © Crown Copyright. Reproduced under the terms of the Open Government Licence (OGL). http://www.nationalarchives.gov.uk/doc/open-government-licence/version/3

Due to the nature of the web, we cannot guarantee the content or links of any site mentioned. We strongly recommend that teachers check websites before using them in the classroom.

Author Jean Evans and Charlotte Lucy Davies Spiers
Editorial team Rachel Morgan, Jenny Wilcox, Kate Pedlar and Elizabeth Evans
Series designer Neil Salt
Designer Anna Oliwa
Illustrator Jim Peacock/Beehive illustration
Digital development Hannah Barnett, Phil Crothers and MWA Technologies Private Ltd

Every effort has been made to trace copyright holders for the works reproduced in this book, and the publishers apologise for any inadvertent omissions.

CONTENTS

Introduction	4
Using the CD-ROM	5
Curriculum links	6
About the book and author	7
Guided reading	8
Shared reading	11
Phonics & spelling	15
Plot, character & setting	17
Talk about it	22
Get writing	26
Assessment	31

INTRODUCTION

Read & Respond provides teaching ideas related to a specific children's book. The series focuses on best-loved books and brings you ways to use them to engage your class and enthuse them about reading.

The book is divided into different sections:

- **About the book and author:** gives you some background information about the book and the author.
- **Guided reading:** breaks the book down into sections and gives notes for using it with guided reading groups. A bookmark has been provided on page 10 containing comprehension questions. The children can be directed to refer to these as they read.
- **Shared reading:** provides extracts from the children's book with associated notes for focused work. There is also one non-fiction extract that relates to the children's book.
- **Phonics & spelling:** provides phonics and spelling work related to the children's book so you can teach these skills in context.
- **Plot, character & setting:** contains activity ideas focused on the plot, characters and the setting of the story.
- **Talk about it:** has speaking and listening activities related to the children's book. These activities may be based directly on the children's book or be broadly based on the themes and concepts of the story.
- **Get writing:** provides writing activities related to the children's book. These activities may be based directly on the children's book or be broadly based on the themes and concepts of the story.
- **Assessment:** contains short activities that will help you assess whether the children have understood concepts and curriculum objectives. They are designed to be informal activities to feed into your planning.

The activities follow the same format:

- **Objective:** the objective for the lesson. It will be based upon a curriculum objective, but will often be more specific to the focus being covered.
- **What you need:** a list of resources you need to teach the lesson, including digital resources (printable pages, interactive activities and media resources, see page 5).
- **What to do:** the activity notes.
- **Differentiation:** this is provided where specific and useful differentiation advice can be given to support and/or extend the learning in the activity. Differentiation by providing additional adult support has not been included as this will be at a teacher's discretion based upon specific children's needs and ability, as well as the availability of support.

The activities are numbered for reference within each section and should move through the text sequentially – so you can use the lesson while you are reading the book. Once you have read the book, most of the activities can be used in any order you wish.

USING THE CD-ROM

Below are brief guidance notes for using the CD-ROM. For more detailed information, please click on the '?' button in the top right-hand corner of the screen.

The program contains the following:
- the extract pages from the book
- all of the photocopiable pages from the book
- additional printable pages
- interactive on-screen activities
- media resources.

Getting started

Put the CD-ROM into your CD-ROM drive. If you do not have a CD-ROM drive, phone Scholastic Customer Services on 0845 6039091.

- For Windows users, the install wizard should autorun. If it fails to do so, then navigate to your CD-ROM drive and follow the installation process.
- For Mac users, copy the disk image file to your hard drive. After it has finished copying, double click it to mount the disk image. Navigate to the mounted disk image and run the installer. After installation, the disk image can be unmounted and the DMG can be deleted from the hard drive.
- To install on a network, see the ReadMe file located on the CD-ROM (navigate to your drive).

To complete the installation of the program you need to open the program and click 'Update' in the pop-up. Please note – this CD-ROM is web-enabled and the content will be downloaded from the internet to your hard drive to populate the CD-ROM with the relevant resources. This only needs to be done on first use after this you will be able to use the CD-ROM without an internet connection. If at any point any content is updated, you will receive another pop-up upon start-up when there is an internet connection.

Main menu

The main menu is the first screen that appears. Here you can access: terms and conditions, registration links, how to use the CD-ROM and credits. To access a specific book click on the relevant button (only titles installed will be available). You can filter by the drop-down lists if you wish. You can search all resources by clicking 'Search' in the bottom left-hand corner. You can also log in and access favourites that you have bookmarked.

Resources

By clicking on a book on the Main menu, you are taken to the resources for that title. The resources are: Media, Interactives, Extracts and Printables. Select the category and then launch a resource by clicking the play button.

Teacher settings

In the top right-hand corner of the screen is a small 'T' icon. This is the teacher settings area. It is password protected, the password is: login. This area will allow you to choose the print quality settings for interactive activities ('Default' or 'Best') and also allow you to check for updates to the program or re-download all content to the disk via 'Refresh all content'. You can also set up user logins so that you can save and access favourites. Once a user is set up, they can enter by clicking the login link underneath the 'T' and '?' buttons.

Search

You can access an all resources search by clicking the search button on the bottom left of the Main menu. You can search for activities by type (using the drop-down filter) or by keyword by typing into the box. You can then assign resources to your favourites area or launch them directly from the search area.

CURRICULUM LINKS

Section	Activity	Curriculum objectives
Guided reading		Comprehension: To participate in discussion about what is read to them, taking turns and listening to what others say. Comprehension: To explain and discuss their understanding of books, poems and other material, both those that they listen to and those that they read for themselves.
Shared reading	1	Comprehension: To draw on what they already know or on background information and vocabulary provided by the teacher.
	2	Comprehension: To appreciate rhymes and poems. Word reading: To apply phonic knowledge and skills as the route to decode words.
	3	Comprehension: To be introduced to non-fiction that is structured in different ways.
Phonics & spelling	1	Word reading: To respond speedily with the correct sound to graphemes for all 40+ phonemes.
	2	Word reading: To read accurately by blending sounds in unfamiliar words containing GPCs that have been taught.
	3	Transcription: To add prefixes and suffixes using 'ing', 'ed', 'er' and 'est', and 's' or 'es'.
	4	Word reading: To read words with contractions, understanding the role of the apostrophe.
Plot, character & setting	1	Comprehension: To link what they read or hear to their own experiences.
	2	Comprehension: To draw on what they already know or on background information and vocabulary provided by the teacher.
	3	Comprehension: To participate in discussion about what is read to them. Composition: To read their writing aloud, clearly enough to be heard.
	4	Comprehension: To make inferences on the basis on what is being said and done. Composition: To discuss what they have written with the teacher or other children.
	5	Comprehension: To make inferences on the basis of what is being said and done.
	6	Composition: To sequence sentences to form short narratives.
Talk about it	1	Comprehension: To appreciate rhymes and poems, and to recite some by heart.
	2	Comprehension: To become very familiar with key stories, fairy stories and traditional tales, retelling them and considering their particular characteristics.
	3	Composition: To discuss what they have written with the teacher or other pupils.
	4	Comprehension: To listen to and discuss a wide range of poems, stories and non-fiction at a level beyond that at which they can read independently.
	5	Comprehension: To predict what might happen on the basis of what has been read so far.
	6	Comprehension: To explain clearly their understanding of what is read to them. Comprehension: To recognise simple recurring literary language in stories and in poetry.
Get writing	1	Composition: To discuss what they have written with the teacher or other pupils.
	2	Composition: To write sentences by composing a sentence orally before writing it. Comprehension: To link what they read or hear to their own experiences.
	3	Transcription: To spell the days of the week.
	4	Composition: To sequence sentences to form short narratives.
	5	Composition: To make simple additions, revisions and corrections to their writing by proofreading to check for errors in spelling, grammar and punctuation.
	6	Composition: To develop positive attitudes towards and stamina for writing by writing for different purposes.
Assessment	1	Transcription: To write from memory simple sentences dictated by the teacher.
	2	Word reading: To read accurately by blending sounds in unfamiliar words containing GPCs.
	3	Transcription: To name the letters of the alphabet in order.
	4	Comprehension: To explain clearly their understanding of what is read to them.

ALIENS LOVE UNDERPANTS

About the book

First published in 2007, *Aliens Love Underpants* tells the hilarious story of a group of aliens who happen to love underpants. They love everything about them, including their colours, patterns and shapes. Sadly, there are no underpants on the planet where they live and so they zoom towards Earth in their spaceship in search of them. The radar screen blinks and bleeps to let them know when they fly over washing lines full of underpants flapping in the breeze. In a flash they land, rush around collecting underpants of every shape and size, and have great fun holding daring competitions and games involving underpants. But… as soon as Mum appears to bring in the washing, the aliens vanish as quickly as they appeared.

This book will provide children with delightful opportunities to 'laugh their pants off' as they enjoy talking, reading and writing about underpants, and taking part in fun underpants-related activities. The rhyming-couplet pattern of the text will help to develop children's ability to appreciate and experiment with the effects of carefully chosen words and rhyme. The book also provides an opportunity to enter the crazy world of a bunch of fictional quirky aliens, where anything goes – including taking other people's underwear!

For cross-curricular work, children could create artwork around the theme of space; design and technology projects could be to make model spaceships, or tie dye underpants (see Extract 3); make links to science, by investigating different materials for underpants, and comparing the aliens' habitat to the habitats of people and animals on Earth.

About the author

Claire Freedman started her working life as a secretary and had many different jobs before she went to a writing class and discovered her talent for writing. The first story she had published was for a children's magazine. After that there was no stopping her and soon she had over 100 books published, including *George's Dragon*, *Tappity Tap! What Was That?* and the many aliens and underpants titles. She still attends the same writing class today! Claire lives on the Essex coast and has a special office to write in. She likes sailing, walking along the beach and travelling abroad.

About the illustrator

Ben Cort studied illustration at Harrow College and has illustrated over 50 books. He has collaborated on several picture books with Claire, such as *Pirates Love Underpants* and *Monstersaurus*. Other books he has illustrated include *Under the Bed* (which won a Practical Pre-School Silver Award in 2003) and *Super Spud and the Stinky Space Rescue*. He was shortlisted for The English 4–11 Awards for the Best Children's Illustrated Books of 2003. As well as illustrating, Ben is a keen photographer.

Key facts

Aliens Love Underpants

Author: Claire Freedman

Illustrator: Ben Cort

First published: 2007 by Simon and Schuster

Awards: The Richard and Judy prize for children's fiction (2–6 years), 2007

On the stage: developed into a stage show in 2015

GUIDED READING

Introducing the book

Display the front cover of the book before starting to read the story to the children so that they can focus on the illustration in order to make predictions about the content.

Read the title and ask question 1 on the Guided Reading bookmark (page 10). Establish the children's understanding of the meaning of the word 'alien' by inviting them to talk about what they know about them from stories, films and other media sources. Draw attention to the names Claire Freedman and Ben Cort, and establish who is the author and who is the illustrator. (To extend this discussion, find out more about them on page 7.)

Explore the features of the characters on the cover, and identify clues that indicate that they are aliens, such as a single eye in the middle of the forehead, several eyes on long stalks and ears shaped like trumpets. Talk about the underpants they are wearing and ask question 2 on the Guided Reading bookmark to encourage children to focus on the importance of illustration.

Look at the background landscape and identify clues that indicate where the story might be set (on an alien planet?). Turn to the illustration on the back cover and consider what role the spaceship might play in the story. Read the text below this and ask question 6 on the Guided Reading bookmark. Establish that the words are arranged like the verse of a poem and are in rhyme.

Having explored the front and back covers, ask question 3 on the Guided Reading bookmark. Discuss the possibility of having a group of significant characters rather than one main one.

Finally, read the blurb sentence on the back cover and ask question 7 on the Guided Reading bookmark to establish that this promises to be a very amusing story.

First reading

Ensure that your first reading of *Aliens Love Underpants* captures the children's imaginations as they share in a laugh-out-loud, engaging experience that builds upon their initial impressions. Read clearly and expressively, making effective use of the many opportunities for breathing space indicated by ellipses; for example, pause after the word 'surprise' so that children wait with anticipation. Vary vocal tone and body language to build up mood and atmosphere: point around the room to individuals, narrowing the eyes and saying 'YOU…' loudly before pausing as indicated; or hold your arms in the air with joy as you chant 'Oooooh, UNDERPANTS!'; indicate horrors to come by lowering your voice to a secretive whisper, for instance, when warning 'in case an alien still lurks inside, unseen!'; and increase your speed to add atmosphere and mounting excitement as you read 'But quick! Mum's coming'.

Indicate words by moving along them with a finger or pointer as you read. Remember to pause at significant points to ask questions about what might happen next, or to invite children to predict a rhyming word.

As you continue to read, ensure that children understand the text through appropriate comments and queries. For instance, ask questions 8 and 9 on the Guided Reading bookmark to focus on the use of appropriate language. If necessary, explain words such as 'zany', 'radar', 'satsumas', 'bloomers' and 'hilarious'.

Ask questions 10, 11 and 12 on the Guided Reading bookmark to encourage children to discuss how they would feel if aliens came to steal their underpants. Extend this to a conversation about the value of personal possessions and why others should not feel they can take them. Always be prepared

GUIDED READING

to follow the children's comments, interests and ideas when you ask these questions, and encourage respect for differing opinions and aspirations.

Draw attention to the detailed illustrations and discuss how they enhance the story. For example, explore the washing instruction icons on the statues on the aliens' planet, and the names on the stickers on their spaceship. Ask question 4 on the Guided Reading bookmark to initiate discussion about where the aliens might have found this information.

Finally, encourage children to voice their initial impressions of the book.

Beginning, middle and end

Re-read the story, this time focusing on how the author has divided it into three distinct sections, beginning on the home planet, with a journey through space in the middle, and then time on Earth to collect underpants before whizzing off at the end. Ask question 5 on the Guided Reading bookmark and discuss the role of the text and illustrations in identifying the three story settings.

Journey through space

Invite children to share what they know about space and space travel before focusing on the spreads depicting the outside and inside of a spaceship. Consider why spaceships shaped like this are sometimes called flying saucers (pass around examples of saucers if children are not familiar with these now that mugs are more popular than cups and saucers). Ask the children what the text tells us about how the radar reacts to the sight of washing on a line. Consider the uses of the other controls, comparing these to familiar objects such as the gear stick and dashboard controls in a car. Discuss the possible actions of the aliens when they see a line of underpants on the screen.

Rhyme for a reason

Revisit question 6 on the Guided Reading bookmark and the subsequent discussion related to the effect of rhyme in stories. Focus on the importance of this feature in this book. Ask the children to choose a favourite page and read it to them, emphasising the rhyming words as you do so. Read the page again, this time clapping the syllables to enable children to appreciate the rhythm.

Now read the page a third time, but substitute rhyming words with non-rhyming words that have similar meanings; for example, substitute 'parts/races' for 'places/races' on the spread depicting the aliens wearing underpants in silly places. Ask which version had rhyming words and decide as a class which one sounds best.

Laugh your pants off!

Revisit question 7 on the Guided Reading bookmark and recall earlier conclusions that the book must be a funny story. Invite the children to choose their funniest moment from the story. Extend this further by choosing 'funny categories' as a class. Write suggested headings on the board and then scribe the children's ideas underneath. For instance, 'Funniest sentence', 'Funniest word', 'Funniest illustration', 'Funniest alien'. Choose the overall winner in each category.

READ&RESPOND Aliens Love Underpants **9**

SCHOLASTIC
READ & RESPOND
Bringing the best books to life in the classroom

Aliens Love Underpants
by Claire Freedman

Focus on… Meaning

1. What do you think the story might be about by reading the title?

2. How does the illustration on the front cover demonstrate that aliens love underpants?

3. Can you tell if there is a main character in this story by looking at the cover?

Focus on… Organisation

4. What do the aliens know about underpants, and how do you think they know this? Look for clues in the illustrations of the sculptures and flying saucers on the first few pages.

5. Name the three different settings that the story takes place in. What clues did the text and illustrations provide to help you with your answer?

SCHOLASTIC
READ & RESPOND
Bringing the best books to life in the classroom

Aliens Love Underpants
by Claire Freedman

Focus on… Language and features

6. What do the first four lines of text on the back cover tell you about the way the story is written? Do you enjoy reading a story that is in rhyme? Can you say why?

7. What do the words 'zany', 'hilarious' and 'laugh your pants off' on the back cover tell us about the story? Why does it say 'laugh your pants off' instead of 'laugh your head off'?

8. Why does the author use the phrase 'next door's funny game' to describe the washing disappearing?

9. What do the words 'whizzy', 'zinging' and 'zoom' tell you about how the aliens move?

Focus on… Purpose, viewpoints and effects

10. Do the aliens' games sound fun? Which is your favourite?

11. Do you think the aliens should steal underpants?

12. Has anyone ever stole anything of yours? How did you feel?

SHARED READING

Extract 1

- Display and read together an enlarged copy of Extract 1. Invite the children to discuss the information it conveys about the story. Recall previous discussion about a possible main character and ask whether the extract provides any further clues. Consider whether it could be the reader, indicated by the word 'YOU'. Identify the information given in the extract about the aliens.

- Highlight the rhyming words and discuss their position (at the end of the second and final line of each verse). Discuss how the text resembles a poem because of the shape and this regular positioning of rhyming words.

- Together, examine the spelling of the rhyming words and identify phonemes that have different graphemes, for example, 'size/surprise', 'you/knew'. Discuss why 'you' is a common exception word.

- Talk about the purpose of the two ellipses and ask: *Does this pause make you think about what will happen next?*

Extract 2

- Display and read an enlarged copy of Extract 2. Establish that this is the ending of the book and discuss whether it is effective in concluding the story action. Ask questions such as: *Why did the aliens zoom off? Why are they used to leaving fast? Why should you check your underpants before putting them on?*

- Encourage the children to apply existing phonic knowledge to read words such as 'washing' and 'zoom'. Tackle the uncommon word, 'lurks' in the same way, asking children to think of other words that contain the /ur/ phoneme if necessary (for example, 'turn', 'hurt', 'church'). Invite children to highlight as many different words as they can that contain phonemes representing the /ee/ sound.

- Circle the exclamation marks and discuss their effectiveness in these positions.

- Read the two sentences with the contractions, 'Mum's' and 'they're', and then without ('Mum is', 'they are'). Explain that the author uses contractions to keep the rhythm consistent.

Extract 3

- Display an enlarged copy of Extract 3. Explain that it is a fun page about underpants with facts and an activity. Read the 'fascinating facts' together, encouraging children to tackle unfamiliar words such as 'loincloths' and 'bloomers'.

- Establish that the rest of the page is set out as an instruction sheet. Read the list of items needed and consider reasons why an adult might be asked to help.

- Read the first instruction under 'What to do', encouraging children to use their existing phonic knowledge and skills to build up the words. Support them with any words they are still challenged by. Consider the reason for the accompanying illustration. Do the same with the remaining instructions and discuss why they are numbered. You may want to organise a follow-up lesson so that the children can tie dye their own underpants.

READ&RESPOND Aliens Love Underpants **11**

▼ SHARED READING

Extract 1

Aliens love underpants,
Of every shape and size.
But there are no underpants in space,
So here's a big surprise…

When aliens fly down to Earth,
They don't come to meet YOU…
They simply want your underpants –
I'll bet you never knew!

SHARED READING

Extract 2

But quick! Mum's coming out to fetch
The washing in at last.
Wheee! Off the aliens all zoom,
They're used to leaving fast...

So when you put your pants on,
Freshly washed and nice and clean,
Just check in case an alien
Still lurks inside, unseen!

SHARED READING

Extract 3

Underpants facts

- The first underpants were leather loincloths worn by cavemen.
- Jack Stringer holds the record for wearing the most pairs of underpants at once (215 pairs, in June 2010 when he was ten years old).
- A pair of Queen Victoria's silk bloomers once sold for over ten thousand pounds.

How to make designer underpants

- Follow these instructions to create patterns on plain underpants.

You will need:

An adult, pair of white underpants, rubber bands, fabric dye, salt (if asked for in fabric dye's instructions) pan, large bowl.

What to do:

1. Twist a little piece of your underpants into a bunch and fasten it with a rubber band. Repeat until your underpants are covered in tiny bunches.
2. Put your underpants into a bowl of water and make sure they are wet all over.
3. Ask an adult to follow the instructions on the dye packet, mixing the dye in a pan with water.
4. Put the underpants in the pan and ask an adult to heat the pan following the packet's instruction.
5. Allow time to cool, then remove the underpants and rinse until the water runs clear. Take off the rubber bands.
6. Make your underpants even more interesting by sewing fabric scraps, ribbons and lace to them!

PHONICS & SPELLING

1. Missing phonemes

Objective

To respond speedily with the correct sound to graphemes for all 40+ phonemes, including alternative sounds for graphemes.

What you need

A copy of *Aliens Love Underpants*, interactive activity 'Fill the gaps', individual whiteboards.

What to do

- Read *Aliens Love Underpants* to the children and ask them to choose a favourite page. Read out any words on that page that contain a phoneme already taught, such as /oo/ in 'bloomers' or /ee/ in 'green'. (Choose another page for more relevant examples that match children's reading levels if necessary.) Ask the children to write each word on their whiteboards. Discuss the grapheme used to create the phoneme in each case.

- Display interactive activity 'Fill the gaps'. Explain that the aliens have printed letters (graphemes), which make up phonemes, on their underpants.

- Read the instructions and work through two examples together to ensure that the children understand what they are required to do: they need to drag and drop the graphemes from the underpants to complete the words in the baskets at the bottom of the screen, reading aloud the words they have created.

- Allow time for the children to complete the activity in pairs.

- Bring the class together to think of words with alternative graphemes that make the same sound as each grapheme displayed on the underpants. They could write them as pairs of words on their whiteboards: for example, train (interactive activity) and play (alternative choice); church (interactive activity) and bird (alternative choice).

Differentiation

Extension: Challenge pairs of children to write sentences containing the words that they created when they completed the activity.

2. Alien words

Objective

To read accurately by blending sounds in unfamiliar words containing GPCs that have been taught.

What you need

A copy of *Aliens Love Underpants*, interactive activity 'Alien words'.

What to do

- Recall previous activities involving 'alien' words (words which have no meaning); if the children are familiar with this term, discuss why such words are referred to as 'alien'. Write pairs of words on the board, one with the correct spelling and the other as an alien word, for example 'new/nyoo', 'Earth/Urth'. Invite children to identify the correct spelling.

- Explore the illustration in the book of spaceships hurtling through space. Draw the children's attention to the stickers on the largest one.

- Display interactive activity 'Alien words'. Explain that the aliens had been learning to read English words before visiting Earth and wanted to use them as stickers to decorate their spaceships and rockets. However, they got these words mixed up with their own alien words and so their flying saucer is decorated with a mixture of English and alien words.

- Read the interactive activity instruction together. Invite a child to choose an English word to drag and drop onto the correct rocket. Do the same with an alien word.

- Ask children to work in pairs to complete the activity, supporting one another with reading.

Differentiation

Support: Ask children to concentrate on highlighting the six recognisable words.

Extension: Challenge children to find the English words they have identified in a copy of *Aliens Love Underpants*.

READ & RESPOND Aliens Love Underpants **15**

PHONICS & SPELLING

3. Revising suffixes

Objective
To know and apply the spelling rules for using 'ing', 'ed', 'er' and 'est', and for adding 's' or 'es'.

What you need
Copies of *Aliens Love Underpants*, interactive activity 'Which ending?'.

What to do
- Revise or introduce the children to the term 'suffix'. Explain that it is an ending that can be added to a word to create a new word.
- Revise the rules for adding the suffixes 'ing' and 'ed' to regular verbs, and 'er' and 'est' to adjectives (for example, if the word ends in two consonant letters the ending is simply added on). Provide examples such as: 'add/adding/added', 'cold/colder/coldest'.
- Revise the rule for plural endings. (If the ending sounds like /s/ or /z/ it is spelled as 's'; if it sounds like /iz/ it is spelled 'es'.) Again provide examples, such as: 'boats', 'books' and 'shops'; 'foxes', 'churches' and 'princesses'.
- Display screen 1 of interactive activity 'Which ending?'. Read the instruction together to ensure that the children understand what to do. Complete the sentences together on screen.
- Display screen 2 and screen 3 in turn, inviting the children to choose a sentence from each to complete on their whiteboards. Discuss results.
- Allow time for individual completion of the whole activity before discussing the correct suffixes as a class.

Differentiation
Support: Complete only the screen/s relevant to the child's current experience and ability.
Extension: Explore the two words in *Aliens Love Underpants* with suffixes following vowel-consonant endings ('flap/flapping' and 'spot/spotted') and identify the extra letter that has been added (the final consonant has been doubled). Find further examples in other books.

4. Recognising and understanding contractions

Objective
To read words with contractions, understanding the role of the apostrophe.

What you need
Copies of *Aliens Love Underpants*, Extracts 1 and 2, printable page 'Writing contractions'.

What to do
- Revise the meaning of 'contraction'. Display Extract 1 and invite the children to highlight the first contraction (here's). Decide on the two words this contraction represents (here is) and write them on the screen. Ask whether they think the extract sounds better with or without the contraction.
- Repeat with 'I'll (I will) and the two contractions in Extract 2 ('Mum's/Mum is' and 'They're/They are').
- Use contractions in your instructions, asking the children to identify them as they listen (for example, I'm going to ask you to do some work of your own on contractions today; I've prepared some sentences).
- Display printable page 'Writing contractions' and read the instructions. Work through the first sentence on the board together, asking for a volunteer to scribe.
- Read the last two sentences and discuss how the position of the apostrophe in the opening words 'It is not' can create two different contractions.
- Provide each child with a copy of the printable sheet to complete. Ask pairs to compare finished work and discuss any differences.
- Bring the class together to work through the sheet on the board so that the children can self-correct.

Differentiation
Support: Encourage children to concentrate on just the first three sentences.
Extension: Challenge children to compose their own sentences using contractions.

PLOT, CHARACTER & SETTING

1. Accurate adjectives

Objective
To link what they read or hear to their own experiences.

What you need
Copies of *Aliens Love Underpants*, interactive activity 'Favourite underpants', individual whiteboards.

Cross-curricular link
Mathematics

What to do

- Revisit the meaning of 'adjective'. Choose someone to stand at the front of the class and invite the rest of the class to think of adjectives to describe an item of clothing he/she is wearing. Encourage more detailed description by using two adjectives, for example, 'purple, spotted socks'.

- Read *Aliens Love Underpants*, paying particular attention to the alien illustrations. Ask the children to focus on one of these aliens and to write as many adjectives as they can to describe their chosen alien's underpants on their whiteboards.

- Children take turns to read the adjectives back to the class before finding the alien in the book and discussing how accurate the description was.

- Now ask the children to write down adjectives to describe their own favourite pants and allow time for them to read them to the class.

- Display screen 1 of interactive activity 'Favourite underpants' and read the instructions together. Complete the first example as a class, to make sure that the children are aware of what they need to do, before asking them to complete the activity individually.

Differentiation

Support: Hold up underpants with different designs and colours for children to describe them.
Extension: Ask children to design unusual underpants for the aliens, thinking of appropriate adjectives to describe them.

2. The mystery planet

Objective
To explore settings by drawing on what they already know and on provided information.

What you need
Copies of *Aliens Love Underpants*, media resources 'Planets' and 'Spaceships', grey fabric, cardboard tubes and boxes, a variety of underpants, a washing line, pegs, PVA glue, tape.

Cross-curricular links
Drama, art and design, science

What to do

- Recall previous story settings together before discussing the settings for this story (an alien planet, the flying saucer in space, and Earth).

- Ask what the children already know about planets. Use media resource 'Planets', to extend the discussion. Explain that Pluto often appears in pictures of the solar system but is too small to be a planet, and is now called a 'dwarf planet'.

- Look at the illustrations of the aliens' planet in *Aliens Love Underpants* and point out unusual features, such as the sculptures of underpants.

- Explore the images on media resource 'Spaceships'. Invite children's contributions to the discussion. Ask: *Is this an alien spaceship, or a rocket for astronauts?*

- Divide the children into groups to create the different settings. For example, create the planet's surface by draping grey fabric over large boxes; the sculptures of underpants on top of plinths; the inside of the spaceship by arranging small chairs; a washing line of underpants some distance away.

- Allow each group to take turns to visit each area in order to dramatise the story scenario. Encourage children to explore and modify their dramatisations before performing them to the class.

- After each performance ask the audience to comment on the success of the production. Remind children to be positive and constructive.

PLOT, CHARACTER & SETTING

3. I am an alien

Objectives
To participate in discussion about what is read to them, taking turns and listening to others.
To read their writing aloud, clearly enough to be heard by their peers and the teacher.

What you need
A copy of *Aliens Love Underpants*, media resource 'Aliens', printable page 'I am an alien'.

What to do
- Recall previous discussions about the main characters in stories. Ask the children if they think there is a main character in this story, or whether several characters share equal importance. Consider whether the aliens, or the family whose washing they steal, play a greater part in the story.
- Explore the illustrations of the aliens in the book and images from media resource 'Aliens'. Invite children to choose a favourite alien to describe to the class. Talk about similarities and differences between these aliens chosen by different children.
- Ask the children the sort of alien they would like to be, and suggest that you pretend to transform them all by chanting a magic spell.
- Display printable page 'I am an alien' and explain to the children that this page is to help them to plan the sort of alien they would like to become. Read the headings in each box together and speculate as to some of the words they might want to include.
- Allow time for children to discuss this in pairs before filling in individual copies of the page.
- Invite children to describe their alien character to the class, using their notes for support.

Differentiation
Extension: Challenge groups of children of similar ability to create a family of aliens, allocating roles and introducing themselves to the class with a short description of the part they play in family life.

4. Responding to the alien invasion

Objectives
To make inferences on the basis of what is being said and done.
To discuss what they have written.

What you need
Copies of *Aliens Love Underpants*, individual copies of printable page 'Alien invasion'.

What to do
- Recall initial discussions about the characters in the story and how the focus is mainly on the aliens.
- Discuss the actions of the other characters featured: Mum taking in washing, the boy checking for aliens in his underpants, the cat looking curiously at an alien and the dog chasing one.
- Display printable page 'Alien invasion' and discuss Mum's possible responses to the first question. Explore the book illustrations and text for clues linked to this character: for example, Mum does not appear to have seen any aliens so we can infer that she doesn't know who made the garden a mess.
- Put the children into groups of four with individual copies of the printable sheet. Ask groups to focus on the question for one character at a time recording their joint response individually.
- Bring the groups together and ask members of each group to take turns to read out a different character's response from their question sheet.
- Compare the responses from each group and decide on the most probable for that character.

Differentiation
Support: Encourage children to look at the appropriate illustration while asking them about how each character might be feeling.
Extension: Children take turns to play the role of one of the characters while the others ask questions. Allow children time to prepare their questions.

PLOT, CHARACTER & SETTING

5. Welcome aliens

Objective
To make inferences on the basis of what is being said and done.

What you need
Copies of *Aliens Love Underpants*, photocopiable page 20 'Welcome aliens!', paper, coloured pens.

Cross-curricular link
Art and design

What to do
- Read *Aliens Love Underpants* together again. Encourage the children to compare the lifestyle of the aliens with their own; for example, what they wear and where they live.
- Explore the book's illustrations of aliens landing in the garden and having fun collecting underpants.
- Ask the children how they would feel if they witnessed this invasion. Would they run away or would they try to make friends, perhaps?
- Invite the children to imagine they are hosting a surprise picnic party for the aliens to welcome them to Earth. What would they serve them?
- Make inferences together from textual clues about things that are familiar to the aliens (such as flying saucers, spaceships and planets) and things that they really like (such as underpants and silly games). Ask the children to invent foods based on these inferences, such as sandwiches shaped like underpants, flying saucer biscuits and silly drinks that fizz and pop.
- Put the children into groups to plan a funny picnic for the alien visitors. Provide paper, pens and copies of photocopiable page 20 'Welcome aliens!'.

Differentiation
Support: Encourage children to draw their ideas and support them with labelling items.
Extension: Ask children to make inferences about the conversation the aliens will have about the picnic when they return to their planet.

6. Tell the story

Objective
To sequence sentences to form short narratives.

What you need
Copies of *Aliens Love Underpants*, photocopiable page 21 'Tell the story' (one per group), scissors, glue sticks, large sheets of paper, coloured pens.

Cross-curricular link
Art and design

What to do
- Revise any prior knowledge relating to story structure, recalling the terms 'beginning', 'middle' and 'end', and emphasising the need for sentences to follow a sequence.
- Divide the board into three sections, with the headings 'Beginning', 'Middle' and 'End'. Invite children to suggest key events from this story and to write them on the board in the appropriate section.
- Display an enlarged version of photocopiable page 21 'Tell the story'. Explain that you have muddled the sentence order and need the children to sort it out. Read the sentences together and discuss possible sections to place them in.
- Explain that you would like groups of children to create a pictorial storyboard each, using the sentences. Supply each group with a copy of the photocopiable sheet along with glue sticks, scissors, coloured pens, and a large sheet of paper.
- Suggest that the children stick the sentences onto the paper, spaced well apart, or in boxes, but following a sequence. The children should then add their own artwork.
- Display the finished work for groups to explore and discuss which is most effective.

Differentiation
Support: Children identify the opening and closing sentences, cut these out and place at least four of the other sentences in between.
Extension: Invite children to create a similar storyboard, about a different story.

READ&RESPOND *Aliens Love Underpants* **19**

▼ PLOT, CHARACTER & SETTING

Welcome aliens!

- Use this page to plan a surprise picnic party for the aliens.

Sandwiches

Type of bread: _____

Sandwich shapes: _____

Fillings: _____

Finger food

Cakes and pastries: _____

Crisps: _____

Biscuits: _____

Fruit and vegetables: _____

Drinks

Hot: _____

Cold: _____

Extra treats

Frozen treats: _____

Jellies: _____

Sweets: _____

Party bag contents

_____

_____

_____

PLOT, CHARACTER & SETTING

Tell the story

- Cut out the boxes.
- Rearrange the sentences in the correct sequence to tell the story.

One day they decided to travel to Earth in spaceships to look for underpants.
They had enormous fun inventing competitions involving the underpants.
Whoosh! The aliens were gone!
They landed in a garden that had lots of underpants hanging on a washing line.
The aliens loved underpants so much that they created tall statues of them.
Remember... always check for aliens hiding in your underpants!
Once upon a time some aliens lived on a planet where there were no underpants.
When they spotted a human they ran to their spaceship.

READ&RESPOND Aliens Love Underpants

TALK ABOUT IT

1. Making patterns

Objective
To appreciate rhymes and poems and to recite some by heart.

What you need
Copies of *Aliens Love Underpants*, Extract 1, interactive activity 'Making patterns'.

Cross-curricular link
Mathematics

What to do

- Read *Aliens Love Underpants* together, focusing on the regular pattern of the words, which are arranged in rhyming couplets. Discuss the satisfying effect this creates.

- Display Extract 1 and read the first verse together. Repeat until the children can remember without looking. Invite someone to highlight the two rhyming words (using the pen tool).

- Read the second verse and do the same.

- Revisit the previous discussion relating to Extract 1 (on contractions, see page 16) and consider how the punctuation supports the reader.

- Display interactive activity 'Making patterns'. Read the instructions and establish which words rhyme. Ask one child to drag and drop the red underpants next to the rhyming words in the first verse.

- The ask the children to drag and drop the blue pants next to the lines that do not rhyme.

- Complete the whole screen and comment on how the pattern made by the underpants matches the pattern made by the rhyming words.

Differentiation

Support: Highlight the rhyming words (using the pen tool) to make it easier for children to match the underpants to the correct words.
Extension: Challenge children to compose two rhyming couplets about the aliens.

2. Down to Earth

Objective
To become very familiar with a story, retelling it and considering its particular characteristics.

What you need
Copies of *Aliens Love Underpants*, a washing line, pegs, a collection of underpants, two old mobile phones.

Cross-curricular link
Drama

What to do

- Read *Aliens Love Underpants* and discuss how this story has a typical structure, with a clear beginning (the aliens deciding to fly to Earth from their planet), middle (the aliens having fun taking underpants from a washing line) and end (the aliens flying home).

- Ask the children to introduce their favourite stories to the class and explain what happens at the beginning, middle and end.

- Talk about the particular characteristics of this story (such as humour, rhyme and fantasy), and think of other stories in this genre.

- Explain that the children will be dramatising the events in the middle of the story.

- Divide into groups to dramatise key alien actions, such as dancing and chanting with delight, taking photographs of each other, playing games and holding competitions.

- Encourage the children to consider and portray the aliens' feelings, ranging from delight at the sight of so many underpants to horror as the neighbour's dog chases them.

- Provide an outdoor area where groups can practise and perform finished scenarios for the rest of the class. Include a washing line suspended safely just above child height, underpants, pegs and old phones. Encourage imaginative language by asking children to pretend to call the aliens back at home with detailed descriptions of underpants.

TALK ABOUT IT

3. Pants-tastic fun day

Objective

To discuss what they have written with the teacher or other children.

What you need

Copies of *Aliens Love Underpants*, a selection of clean children's underpants of various sizes, individual whiteboards.

Cross-curricular link

PE

What to do

- Read the story before focusing on the pages depicting the aliens playing with underpants and inventing crazy competitions.

- Discuss some of the uses the aliens have for underpants as a class, such as hiding places and slides, and write these on the board.

- Establish the meaning of 'competition' by asking children to share experiences of taking part in one.

- Explore the author's imaginative language, for example 'super-whizzy', 'zinging', 'pants-tastic' and 'pingy'. Discuss the meanings of these words. Suggest working in groups to plan a 'pants-tastic' fun day with silly games and crazy competitions.

- Spend time as a class discussing possible quirky titles for games, such as: 'Pass the pants'; 'Crazy counts' (involving pegging as many pants to a washing line as they can in one minute); 'Whopping hopping' races with a pair of pants hanging on one foot; or dizzy dances entitled 'Ants in my pants!'.

- Put the class into groups to make plans for their games. Explain that they should make up a title for each event and write this on their whiteboards.

- Bring the class together to discuss the game titles the groups have written down.

- Plan time to enjoy some of the children's ideas as a fun lesson, using a selection of underpants.

4. Signs and symbols

Objective

To explore and discuss the meanings of laundering symbols and instructions.

What you need

Copies of *Aliens Love Underpants*, children's clothes displaying a range of laundering symbols, printable page 'Washing instructions for underpants', individual whiteboards.

What to do

- Ask the children why we wash our clothes and how we do this. Hold up a delicate item of clothing, such as a wool jumper, and a robust item, such as some cotton underpants. Discuss whether we should wash both of these items in the same way. Draw attention to the laundering labels and talk about how helpful they could be.

- Divide the children into groups to explore small piles of clothing and find as many different laundering symbols as possible to write on whiteboards.

- Bring the class together to share the symbols discovered and speculate about what they mean.

- Explore the pages from *Aliens Love Underpants* that include illustrations of underpants statues and explore the symbols etched into the statue plinths. Notice how these also occur on the book covers the aliens are reading. Discuss why these aliens need to understand the symbols.

- Display the laundering symbols on printable page 'Washing instructions for underpants'. Explain that these symbols appear on the statues. Ask children to guess what they mean and then reveal the right-hand columns to see how many guesses were correct.

Differentiation

Support: Draw children's attention to helpful clues, such as hands and irons.
Extension: Ask children to design washing instruction sheets for aliens.

READ&RESPOND Aliens Love Underpants 23

TALK ABOUT IT

5. New endings

Objective
To predict what might happen on the basis of what has been read so far.

What you need
Copies of *Aliens Love Underpants*, sentences from photocopiable page 25 'Change the ending' cut out and stuck onto card.

Cross-curricular link
Drama

What to do
- Discuss the story ending and decide whether it is a good one. Encourage the children to give reasons for their answers.
- Talk about how the children might feel if the ending had been different. Perhaps they still think they would prefer the original ending? Explain that they are going to explore different events that could alter the ending to see if their feelings change.
- Divide the class into six groups and provide each group with one of the cards from photocopiable page 25 'Change the ending'. Ask the children to read the event depicted on their card. Explain that this event takes place just after the story ends in the book, leading on to an entirely different ending.
- Invite the groups to dramatise their ideas about how the story ending could change after their new event takes place. Encourage them to try out their individual suggestions and choose the most effective. Ask whether they prefer the ending they have finally created or the original.
- Bring the class together and allow each group to perform their new ending.
- Decide on a favourite ending by a vote of hands (include the original ending in this).

Differentiation
Extension: Challenge children to invent alternative story endings without using the cards supplied.

6. Making comparisons

Objectives
To understand how making comparisons can make descriptions more clear.
To recognise simple recurring literary language in stories and in poetry.

What you need
Copies of *Aliens Love Underpants*, interactive activity 'Making comparisons', fruit and vegetables, including a satsuma.

What to do
- Read *Aliens Love Underpants*. Revisit the page beginning 'They like them red'.
- Hold up a satsuma from a pile of fruit and vegetables and talk about whether 'orange like satsumas' is a good comparison. Ask children to suggest other orange things the author could have used instead. (If they suggest things like socks or a car, because they have them at home, emphasise that these items occur in other colours and so are not good examples.)
- Discuss how making comparisons (there is no need to use the term 'simile') might help the aliens to learn the language spoken by humans.
- Display screen 1 of interactive activity 'Making comparisons' and read the word 'yellow'. Read the words at the bottom of the screen as a class and choose which pair of words links with yellow. Drag and drop these words into place. Ask if the comparison is appropriate.
- Display screen 2. Explain that 'as' can be used to make comparisons as well as 'like'. Work through the first example together.
- Ask the children to complete the activity in pairs in order to discuss their choices.
- Bring the class together to self-correct their work.

Differentiation
Support: Children could complete screen 1 only.
Extension: Children to write comparisons for the fruit and vegetables available.

TALK ABOUT IT

Change the ending

- Cut out the boxes to form cards for the activity.

The alien jumped out of the drawer and into the boy's underpants! "Gooploberfix?" it asked him.

"Zeezeeplixabron!" squeaked the alien and the boy turned into a statue, still holding out his underpants.

Suddenly a spaceship appeared at the window and the door opened. The alien dragged the boy towards it.

The boy spotted the alien, quickly grabbed the drawer handles and pushed it shut. "Meexillia probsquir!" squeaked a muffled voice.

Mum came running in. "Quick!" she shouted. "The aliens are taking our underpants from the washing line. You must help me to stop them."

The boy grabbed the alien from the drawer. "Hello!" he said. "Can I visit your planet? I will bring lots of underpants."

READ&RESPOND Aliens Love Underpants 25

GET WRITING

1. Book review

Objective

To discuss what they have written with the teacher or other children.

What you need

Copies of *Aliens Love Underpants*, reviews of children's books, printable page 'Book review'.

What to do

- Read *Aliens Love Underpants*. Recall children's initial impressions of the story. Ask if they have changed these opinions after several readings and, if so, why.

- Invite current opinions about the book. Ask: *What is the most enjoyable thing about the book? What do you think of the illustrations? Does the regular rhyme help you to enjoy it more?*

- Explain the purpose of a book review and read some sample reviews of children's favourite books. Explain that their task is to write their own reviews of *Aliens Love Underpants*.

- Display a large copy of printable page 'Book review' and read it together, a section at a time.

- Talk about how it is difficult to comment on the merits or shortcomings of individual alien characters because they all take part in similar events, and only differ in appearance.

- Discuss how the individual settings are linked because they are part of a journey from a planet through space to Earth. Decide whether these settings are effective places to set a story.

- Clarify what is meant by 'rating'.

- Ask the children to fill in a copy of the page as a plan, prior to writing an independent book review.

- Bring the children together to share and discuss their completed reviews.

Differentiation

Support: Ask children to complete the first two sections of the review only.
Extension: Invite children to use another copy of the page to plan reviews for other funny stories.

2. Right and wrong

Objectives

To write sentences by composing orally first. To link what they read or hear to their own experiences.

What you need

Copies of *Aliens Love Underpants*, printable page 'Letter to an alien'.

Cross-curricular link

PSHE

What to do

- Discuss how babies and toddlers often take things without asking because they are too young to understand consequences.

- Encourage the children to share experiences of things of theirs that have been taken without permission. Handle comments sensitively.

- Read *Aliens Love Underpants* together. Discuss the family's feelings when they find their underpants have been taken. Suggest that aliens may not understand human feelings and that is why they do not realise it is wrong to take things from others.

- Display printable page 'Letter to an alien' and read it together. Establish who has written it and the important issues raised (such as taking things without permission, or causing upset to others).

- Talk about how the boy intends to make the aliens understand that what they have done is wrong and to make sure that they do not to repeat their actions.

- Discuss the alien's possible responses to the letter. Will he/she accept the invitation? Will he/she apologise? Will he/she promise to return the underpants?

- Ask pairs of children to write the alien's reply. Encourage them to compose their sentences orally and then modify them if necessary before writing them.

- Invite pairs to read their letters to the class. Decide on the best response to the letter.

26 READ&RESPOND *Aliens Love Underpants*

GET WRITING

3. Photographic and diary records

Objective
To spell the days of the week.

What you need
Copies of *Aliens Love Underpants*, a camera, a video camera, an example of a completed diary, photocopiable page 29 'My photographic and diary record', individual whiteboards.

Cross-curricular link
Computing

What to do

- Read the story and discuss what the aliens might tell their friends when they return home.

- Talk about different ways of recording events, such as taking photographs, making films and writing in diaries. Pass around the example diary and comment on how each page is organised.

- Explore the camera and video camera together and discuss how they work.

- Focus on the illustration in the story of the aliens using a camera and video camera. Ask: *What images might they create?*

- Display photocopiable page 29 'My photographic and diary record'. Explain that it combines two forms of record keeping: images and words.

- Ask the children to write the days of the week on their whiteboards in order. Then write each day on the board so that children can self-check their work.

- Encourage the children to consider things that the aliens would photograph over a week, such as: the arrival and departure of their spaceship; the competitions; and their friends wearing underpants in funny ways.

- Divide the children into pairs, with one copy of the photocopiable sheet per child. Encourage partners to discuss their ideas before filling in their own page.

- Decide, as a class, which alien has created the most interesting account.

4. Writing a sequel

Objective
To sequence sentences to form short narratives.

What you need
Copies of *Aliens Love Underpants*, photocopiable page 21 'Tell the story', interactive activity 'Sequence the story', printable page 'Alien wordbank', coloured whiteboard pens.

Cross-curricular link
Mathematics

What to do

- Read *Aliens Love Underpants*.

- Recall story structure discussions focusing on what happens at the beginning, middle and end.

- Display photocopiable page 21 'Tell the story'. Recall together how the children re-arranged these sentences into the correct sequence to tell the story.

- Display interactive activity 'Sequence the story'. Follow the instructions and complete this revision activity.

- Read the resulting sentence sequence in the chosen order. Ask the children to highlight, in different colours (using the pen tool), the sentences that define the beginning and end of the story.

- Suggest that children write individual sequels to the story. Discuss the meaning of 'sequel' and display printable page 'Alien wordbank' to stimulate initial ideas; for example, the boy may collect rocks and decide to visit the aliens' planet to find new samples.

- Remind the children they must write in sentences using grammar and punctuation.

- Share the completed sequels.

Differentiation

Support: Suggest that children focus on writing three sentences to clearly define the beginning, middle and end of their story.

Extension: Encourage children to use connectives to improve the flow of their stories.

GET WRITING

5. Jumbled words

Objective
To proofread their work.

What you need
Copies of *Aliens Love Underpants*, photocopiable page 30 'Sort the sentences', interactive activity 'Jumbled words'.

What to do
- Read *Aliens Love Underpants* to remind the children of the events sequence.
- Revise punctuation rules for sentences, such as the correct use of capital letters, full stops, question marks and exclamation marks.
- Display the first screen of interactive activity 'Jumbled words' and read the first example together. Ask the children to choose the correct answer from the options in the right-hand column. Discuss their strategies for arriving at this, for example, finding any names mentioned in both, or identifying the words with the capital letter starting the sentence and the full stop ending it. Continue working through examples to ensure the children understand the activity requirement.
- Display photocopiable page 30, 'Sort the sentences'. The children will need to work out the word order themselves and write the sentences down as a story.
- Ask the children to complete the interactive activity before supplying individual copies of the photocopiable sheet for them to complete.
- Emphasise the need to proofread their written work to check for errors.
- Go through both activities as a class so that the children can self-correct their work.

Differentiation
Support: Ask children to concentrate on completing the first screen and the first three sentences on the photocopiable sheet.
Extension: Invite children to write jumbled sentences and challenge partners to rewrite them.

6. Writing instructions

Objective
To write for different purposes.

What you need
Copies of *Aliens Love Underpants*, printable page 'How to make an edible alien', media resource 'Fruit and vegetable aliens', children's cookery books.

Cross-curricular link
Design and technology

What to do
- Read *Aliens Love Underpants* aloud to the children. Ask them to pay attention to the alien's appearance.
- Invite individuals to describe an alien from memory. Check the illustrations together for accuracy.
- Recall discussions about making comparisons, focusing on the description of underpants as being 'orange like satsumas' (see Activity 6 'Making comparisons' on page 24). Ask children to compare the story aliens with different fruits and vegetables.
- Explore the images of edible aliens in media resource 'Fruit and vegetable aliens', before suggesting making edible fruit and vegetable aliens.
- Discuss the way recipes are presented in child-friendly cookery books.
- Display printable page 'How to make an edible alien' and read it together. Ask children to draw their alien in the first box; write the ingredients and equipment needed and compose clear step-by-step instructions. Provide each child with a copy of the sheet to complete.
- Share recipes to decide which would be most fun to make and which instructions easiest to follow.

Differentiation
Support: Concentrate on writing labels for drawings of ingredients and equipment.
Extension: Invite children to compile a vegetarian cookery book using their recipes.

GET WRITING

My photographic and diary record

- Write the days of the week in the first column.
- Draw a picture of the photograph in the second column.
- Write a sentence about the photograph in the third column.

Day	Picture	Description
Sunday		

READ & RESPOND Aliens Love Underpants **29**

▼ GET WRITING

Sort the sentences

- Read the words in the boxes.
- Rewrite them as sentences to tell the story.

{ 1. on a far off planet. some aliens lived Once upon a time }

_____

{ 2. shape and size. of every They loved underpants }

_____

{ 3. to Earth They flew down in a spaceship. }

_____

{ 4. and put them on. from washing lines They grabbed underpants }

_____

{ 5. with the underpants. their distant planet They flew back to }

_____

{ 6. wondered where their The people on Earth underpants had gone! }

_____

ASSESSMENT

1. Listen and remember!

Objective
To write from memory simple sentences dictated by the teacher.

What you need
Prepared sentences, individual whiteboards.

What to do
- Prepare four sentences for dictation linked to *Aliens Love Underpants*, using words that include GPCs and common exception words taught so far, such as: '**Once some** aliens landed on Earth'; '**We** know that **the** aliens **love** underpants **because we** have read about them'; '**Today the** aliens **said** that they might **come to school to** visit this class'; '**I** hope **you** have **your** underpants well hidden under **your clothes**!' (Common exceptions are highlighted in bold.)
- Choose five common exception words that the children have covered so far. Ask them to write them on their whiteboards (see list in the 2014 National Curriculum for English, Appendix 1, for examples). Discuss the correct spelling of these words and write them on the board for self-correction.
- Explain that you have made up four sentences about the aliens, and you want the children to listen carefully and then write the sentences on their whiteboards.
- Read out the first sentence slowly and clearly. Allow time for children to finish writing before asking them to swap their board with a partner.
- Write the sentence on the board and allow time for partners to identify any errors in the sentence.
- Wipe the boards and repeat with the next sentence.
- Assess by observing the children as they write and check each other's work.

Differentiation
Support: Dictate one sentence at an appropriate level.

2. Choose the answer

Objective
To read accurately by blending sounds in unfamiliar words containing taught GPCs.

What you need
A copy of *Aliens Love Underpants*; interactive activity 'Remembering the story'.

What to do
- Read *Aliens Love Underpants* to the class, asking the questions from interactive activity 'Remembering the story' at appropriate points as you go along (without displaying the screens at this stage).
- Revise some of the GPCs already taught by writing a word on the board, underlining the grapheme for a particular phoneme, for example, 'train', and then asking for examples of other words which have the same GPC. Now ask for words with examples of alternative graphemes for the same phoneme (spade, tray).
- Display screen 1 of the interactive activity and read the first question together. Invite individuals to read the three options.
- Ask the children to read the words 'train', 'holiday' and 'space' aloud and identify the common phoneme (/ai/). Discuss how three different graphemes have been used to represent this phoneme. Ask for further examples of words that share the same phoneme. Invite a child to circle the answer chosen by the class. If any child disagrees, refer to the story for confirmation.
- Undertake individual assessments using this activity while discussions and instructions are fresh in the children's minds. For each question ask the child to identify the common phoneme and different graphemes that have been used.

Differentiation
Support: Complete the first five screens only, supporting with reading where necessary.
Extension: Ask children to compose similar question-and-answer activities, using examples of GPCs and focusing on a favourite story.

ASSESSMENT

3. Alphabetical order

Objective
To name the letters of the alphabet in order.

What you need
Copies of *Aliens Love Underpants*, alphabet displays (such as bunting, charts or friezes) depicting upper and lower case letters, interactive activities 'Alphabetical order (1)' and 'Alphabetical order (2)'.

What to do
- Revise letter names and alphabetical order with the class by asking the children to read out the letters by name, in order, from the alphabet display.
- Instruct the children to close their eyes and listen while you call out a letter name. Challenge them to say the name of the letter that comes before it in the alphabet, and the one that comes after it. Ask them to open their eyes and check their answer by locating the letter on an alphabet display.
- Display 'Alphabetical order (1)' and work through it together as revision prior to completing the assessment activity. Discuss strategies for words that begin with the same letters, and those with the same two initial letters.
- Explain that you have a similar activity entitled 'Alphabetical order (2)', which has words from the story arranged in random order. Ask the children to complete this activity individually. (If they need to wait for access to a computer, suggest that pairs of children choose a sentence from the story and arrange the words into alphabetical order.)
- Allow time for individuals to complete the activity before bringing the class together to share their responses.

Differentiation
Support: Assess children on their ability to complete the first two screens; these words all start with different letters.

4. Read and understand

Objective
To explain clearly their understanding of what is read to them.

What you need
Extracts 1 and 2, individual copies of printable page 'Read and understand'.

What to do
- Display Extract 1 and recall previous discussions about this text. Read it aloud and pose questions about the words used, such as: *Which adjective describes the surprise?* (big) *Which word describes how aliens feel about underpants?* (love) Ask children to highlight the 'joining' words that provide continuity between lines (but, so). Query the purpose of punctuation, such as the three dots (ellipsis) at the end of the line, and the apostrophe in the word 'here's'.
- Explain that you are going to challenge the children to answer similar questions about Extract 2 to see how well they understand the story, and the words and punctuation the author uses.
- Display Extract 2 and read it together. Leave this on display and provide each child with a copy of printable page 'Read and understand' to complete. Read through the questions with them before starting, but do not discuss them this time.
- While they are working, visit the children individually to question them about what they are writing, rewording your questions if their responses indicate a lack of understanding.
- When all children have completed the activity, bring the class together. Read the questions one by one and discuss the children's responses.
- Assess the objective through the results of the activity and oral answers given.

Differentiation
Support/Extension: Modify questions to provide the appropriate level of challenge related to the children's current attainment.